Aparna Ravichandran
S.G.R. Prakash

Performance of RIC Hearing Aids in Sloping SN Hearing Loss

Madhav Tamsekar
Aparna Ravichandran
S.G.R. Prakash

Performance of RIC Hearing Aids in Sloping SN Hearing Loss

A Comparative Study

LAP LAMBERT Academic Publishing

Impressum / Imprint

Bibliografische Information der Deutschen Nationalbibliothek: Die Deutsche Nationalbibliothek verzeichnet diese Publikation in der Deutschen Nationalbibliografie; detaillierte bibliografische Daten sind im Internet über http://dnb.d-nb.de abrufbar.
Alle in diesem Buch genannten Marken und Produktnamen unterliegen warenzeichen-, marken- oder patentrechtlichem Schutz bzw. sind Warenzeichen oder eingetragene Warenzeichen der jeweiligen Inhaber. Die Wiedergabe von Marken, Produktnamen, Gebrauchsnamen, Handelsnamen, Warenbezeichnungen u.s.w. in diesem Werk berechtigt auch ohne besondere Kennzeichnung nicht zu der Annahme, dass solche Namen im Sinne der Warenzeichen- und Markenschutzgesetzgebung als frei zu betrachten wären und daher von jedermann benutzt werden dürften.

Bibliographic information published by the Deutsche Nationalbibliothek: The Deutsche Nationalbibliothek lists this publication in the Deutsche Nationalbibliografie; detailed bibliographic data are available in the Internet at http://dnb.d-nb.de.
Any brand names and product names mentioned in this book are subject to trademark, brand or patent protection and are trademarks or registered trademarks of their respective holders. The use of brand names, product names, common names, trade names, product descriptions etc. even without a particular marking in this works is in no way to be construed to mean that such names may be regarded as unrestricted in respect of trademark and brand protection legislation and could thus be used by anyone.

Coverbild / Cover image: www.ingimage.com

Verlag / Publisher:
LAP LAMBERT Academic Publishing
ist ein Imprint der / is a trademark of
OmniScriptum GmbH & Co. KG
Heinrich-Böcking-Str. 6-8, 66121 Saarbrücken, Deutschland / Germany
Email: info@lap-publishing.com

Herstellung: siehe letzte Seite /
Printed at: see last page
ISBN: 978-3-659-12850-9

Zugl. / Approved by: Hyderabad, India, Osmania University, Diss.., 2013

ACKNOWLEDGMENTS

I would like to thank Lord Ganesh for his love and blessings on me, giving me strength to finish this work and also showing me the right way, thanks for giving everything that I could ever wish for.

I profoundly thank my guide **Mrs. Aparna Ravichandran**, Lecturer (Speech and Hearing), Ali Yavar Jung National Institute for the Hearing Handicapped, Southern Regional Centre, for her valuable suggestions, constructive comments and fruitful discussions and extreme patience throughout my work

I profusely thank **Dr. S.G.R. Prakash**, Reader and Assistant Director AYJNIHH, SRC for giving me permission and opportunity to undertake this study and for immense support and encouragement throughout my academics.

I thank all **participants** for their kind co-operation without which this study could not have been possible.

My sincere thanks to all my teaching and non-teaching staff at AYJNIHH, SRC, secundrabad who have supported me in completing my Bachelors Program.

My **Loving Mother**, U has been a great unconditional support, an aide, a crutch & god's greates gift to me!! I am greatful ever so much "**To you I humbly owe what I am today...No words would be enough to express what my pride & joy is in being your son**" To the very end of my existence, I will love you. Thank you **Aai** for everything. **You** are my backbone for my survival......

*Dear **parents** I have no words to convey my love & gratitude towards you both. You have taken all the pains and sorrows to give me best of everything you can. Love you **Aai & Dada.***

Thanks to all those whose names I might have missed out by mistake, thank you one and all.....................

TABLE OF CONTENTS

LIST OF TABLES

LIST OF FIGURES

CHAPTER I
INTRODUCTION

"To hear is as natural and effortless occurrence as it is invisible, man could ask himself how breathing keeps him physically alive as how hearing keeps him psychologically alive" (Levins,1996).

Communication is the process of exchanging information and sharing the ideas to convey meaning which involves speaker and listener. Speaker decodes the message and listener encodes the message to understand the information through listening. So, for successful and effective communication hearing and speech are essential.

Hearing is a critical sense that is necessary for the development and maintenance of auditory skills important for communication. Although the ability to hear normally is taken for granted by most human beings, it is common to see that the sense of hearing is severely impaired or lost in a considerable portion of population, the well-being of the organism is severely affected though not threatened.

Hearing impairment is a loss in hearing sensitivity due to underlying pathological conditions resulting in reversible (conductive hearing loss) and irreversible (sensorineural hearing loss) hearing losses. Sensorineural hearing loss not only causes the reduction in the auditory sensitivity, but also impairs the ability to perceive one or more of the speech parameters.

Hearing aids are electro-acoustic devices used for the amplification of sound. It is a boon for the individuals with hearing impairment who experience difficulty in listening situations & cannot be helped by either medical or surgical intervention. The main function of hearing aid is to amplify sounds to a degree, and which will enable a hearing impaired person to utilize his/her residual hearing in an effective manner (Staab, & Lybarger,1994). Fitting of hearing aid is not only for better hearing but also to improve the quality of life (Nikam, 2003). In the past decades, majority of the hearing aid dispensing centres prescribe hearing aids either with ear mould (soft/hard) or with ear tips.

American Speech-Language-Hearing Association (ASHA, 1988) asserts that amplification should provide audibility and comfort for soft and average input levels, and tolerance for high input levels. The primary goal of current hearing aid fitting strategies is to make the speech signal audible in those regions where the sensitivity is reduced, and in the case of high-frequency hearing loss this means providing high-frequency amplification.

Various methods have been attempted to improve speech understanding in persons with high-frequency hearing losses while maintaining acceptable physical appearance and comfort. Completely in the canal (CIC) and In the canal (ITC) instruments can offer cosmetic advantages; however, occlusion effects are often present and can be problematic. The occlusion effect has been documented as a consistent problem when it comes to maximizing satisfaction with conventional hearing aid fittings (Dillon, 2001; Kiessling, Margolf-Hackl, & Gellar, 2001). Sweetow, & Pirzanski (2003) reported occlusion and ampclusion effects in 28% to 65% of hearing aid wearers. The occlusion effect is the sensation of the increased loudness especially in low frequencies that a person experiences to self-generated sounds such as vocalization, chewing and swallowing. Ampclusion is the combination of low frequency amplification and the occlusion effect (Painton, 1993).

6

The hearing aid users frequently complain of unnatural sound quality of their voice and other internally generated sounds such as chewing and swallowing. One of the most common complaints, particularly among individuals with normal or near normal low frequency hearing is that their own voices sounding bloomy, hollow, or muffled which is often due to the effect of occluding the ear canal. Although such complaints sometimes results from sub-optimal hearing aid settings, they also may be associated with a significant occlusion created by the hearing aid shell or ear mould (Mueller, Bright, & Northern, 1996; Painton, 1993; Kuk, & Ludvigsen, 2002).

For some closed vowels, occluding the external ear using a shallow insertion depth can result in levels of 100dBSPL or greater within the canal (Killion, Wilber, & Gudmundsen, 1988). This energy is centred primarily in the low frequencies, with the peak of occlusion effect typically occurring in the range of 200 to 500 Hz (Mueller, 2003). The magnitude of the occlusion effect varies among individuals, with typical values ranging around 12 to 16 dB, but in some cases as great as 25 to 30 dB (Mueller, Bright, & Northern, 1996; MacKenzie, Ricketts, & Konkle, 2004). Patient dissatisfaction resulting from the occlusion effect can lead to inconsistent hearing aid use or outright rejection.

Individuals with near-normal low frequency hearing sensitivity and considerable hearing loss in the frequencies above approximately 2000 Hz have historically been dissatisfied with traditional hearing aids because of complaints related to the low frequencies being too loud (Otto, 2005; Flynn, Obeling, & Johanson, 2006). This perception could be due to over amplification of the low frequencies and/or the occlusion effect, the build-up of sound pressure in the residual ear canal that occurs when body-conducted sound is trapped by a hearing aid or ear mould (Killion et al, 1988; Mueller, 2003).

The dilemma of over amplification in the low frequencies is easily overcome by frequency-specific gain controls available in modern hearing aids. However, complaints related to the occlusion effect still persist with traditional hearing aids, either in-the-ear or when coupled with an ear mould.

Complaints of occlusion are typically alleviated by introduction of larger vents in the shell of in-the-ear hearing aids or in ear moulds. However, larger vents bring with them the increased possibility of feedback, in turn leading to a restriction of achievable gain. An open-canal hearing aid is a relatively new design coupling a smaller behind-the-ear (BTE) or on-the-ear (OTE) hearing aid to the user's ear canal via a non-occluding signal delivery system. The goal of such coupling is to ameliorate complaints of occlusion.

Manufacturers are able to use this simple acoustic solution in today's hearing aids due to the successful integration of digital feedback management. Feedback, with the aperture of the ear canal open, would indeed be the primary factor limiting gain in open-canal devices in the absence of management algorithms. With non-occluding coupling; small size, and successful feedback management; open-canal devices have rapidly gained popularity with clinicians and patients alike. Most audiologists have several open canal models available within their product lines. Hearing aid users have reported a greater satisfaction level with or preference for open canal aids relative to their old or current hearing aids in several studies (Otto, 2005; Flynn, Obeling, & Johnson, 2006). Taylor (2006) reported that significantly higher satisfaction ratings for open-canal than non-open canal hearing aids in regard to the quality of their own voice, phone comfort, sound localization and appearance in two groups of experienced hearing aid users. However, overall rating in satisfaction with open-canal and non-open canal instrument did not differ significantly.

The more recent trend in the development of open fit instruments is to relocate the receiver from a BTE device to the wearer's ear canal. It is widely believed that this configuration is superior in terms of maximum available gain to BTE's that house both receiver and speaker are coupled to the wearer's ear via a thin sound tube. The greater distance between the microphone and receiver increases attenuation in the feedback path (Ross, & Cirmo, 1980). In recent years, there has been an increasing trend toward BTE hearing aids, including receiver-in-canal (RIC) instrument.

Fig1.1 Receiver in the canal hearing aid

Receivers in the canal hearing aid also known as RIC have been introduced by hearing aid industry. A receiver in canal hearing aid is a hearing instrument in which the receiver is separated from the body of hearing instrument and placed in the user's ear canal. Improved digital signal processing (DSP) technology has made open fittings possible for a larger portion of various hearing loss configuration. This hearing aid consists of a small, non-occluding, non custom ear tip placed in the ear canal. RIC hearing aids can be effective in addressing end-user concerns such as cosmetic appeal, wearer comfort and occlusion. (Gnewikow & Moss, 2006).

Receiver in the canal hearing aids reduces the occlusion effect (i.e. the hollowness of voice), improves sound quality of the wearer's own voice, and improves localization ability.

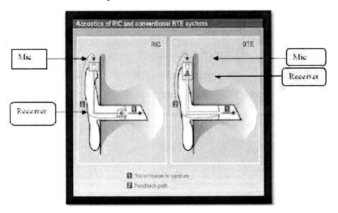

Figure 1.2 Pathway of sound in RIC and conventional BTE hearing aids.

The purported advantages of open canal (OC) hearing aids suggest that these devices may be valuable for individuals with high-frequency hearing loss. The reduction or elimination of the occlusion effect, a more comfortable physical fit, and the relatively inconspicuous appearance afforded by OC hearing aids have the potential to increase user satisfaction. Although, these hearing aids were present since a decade, there is a recent rise of behind the ear (BTE) hearing aid market share.

In general, patients with high frequency (sloping) hearing loss experience difficulty with speech understanding in background noise and for soft or high-pitched voices. However, in quiet situations, mild-to-moderately hearing-impaired patients often exhibit little or no difficulty in understanding speech due to the audibility of a significant portion of lower-frequency speech phonemes. Although the reduction in audibility of high-frequency information can be significantly handicapping, these patients are often hesitant to use hearing aids due to the perceived disadvantages of traditional hearing aids. Visibility, fit, and comfort have been identified as three primary factors that can affect a person's satisfaction and acceptance of amplification.

NEED FOR STUDY

Traditional tube or IROS (Ipsi-lateral routing of signal) with behind-the-ear (BTE) fittings can alleviate occlusion and insertion loss, but may be cosmetically unappealing and present feedback concerns due to the open feedback loop. Resolving or minimizing this issue is considered necessary for the successful use of hearing aids and for improving satisfaction with amplification. Fitting patients who have moderately severe sensorineural hearing losses with appropriate amplification has long been problematic. In general, in quiet situations, these patients often exhibit little or no difficulty in understanding speech due to the audibility of a significant portion of lower-frequency speech phonemes but the voiceless consonants like /t/, /p/, /k/, /f/, /s/ and /ch/ are often missed, they experience greater difficulty with speech understanding in presence of background noise and also for soft or high pitched voice and this reduction in audibility of high-frequency information can impair speech perception.

In conventional BTE's, because the hearing aids are coupled with ear tube and ear mould, there will be acoustic modification of the input signal which would affect speech intelligibility & quality of amplified sound (Dillon, 2001). However in RIC hearing aids, it is coupled with a thin wire and receiver due to which the acoustic modification of the input signal is expected to be negligible. Also since the receiver of the RIC hearing aid is placed within the ear canal the electrical to acoustic conversion is taking place inside the ear canal without any modification to the input signal & results in natural sound quality (Kuk, & Backgaard, 2008). Since the receiver is placed apart from

11

microphone of RIC there is less feedback compared to conventional BTE and also RIC open fit. Technology offers relief from occlusion (Kuk, & Backgaard, 2008).

Recently, in India there is an increase in number of hearing aid prescriptions with RIC. Although there are anecdotal and empirical reports from hearing aid manufacturer of increased patient satisfaction with open fittings, limited data exist outside of the hearing aid industry. Product popularity and laboratory evidence do not equate to real-world satisfaction and benefit in everyday listening situations. In recent years, evidence-based practice has pointed out the need for effectiveness as well as efficiency studies. With the recent growth in the OC hearing aid market, there is a need to investigate the performance of RIC hearing aids.

While the numerous advantages of open-canal hearing aids over traditional fittings have been theorized, little research has been conducted to verify these benefits. The high dispensing rate must be validated by evidence supporting the advantages of open-canal hearing instrument fitting including improved comfort of fit, cosmetics, sound quality, and localization, ease of repair/maintenance, intelligibility, high frequency gain and reduction of the occlusion effect. The clinicians need to critically examine the validity of hearing instrument products before prescribing the technology. Hence, the current study was undertaken to focus on such factors of RIC hearing aids.

AIM OF THE STUDY

The present study was aimed to measure the performance of digital hearing aids with receiver in the canal (i.e. open fit) in individuals with high frequency (sloping) sensorineural hearing loss and compare their performance with traditional occluded fittings (i.e. hearing aids with ear tip & hearing aids with ear mould) in quiet, SNR +5dB & SNR 0dB conditions.

OBJECTIVES OF THE STUDY

The present study was designed with the following objectives,

1. To measure & compare the speech identification scores of subjects fitted with ear tips, ear moulds, and RIC hearing aids in quiet condition.
2. To measure & compare the speech identification scores of subjects fitted with ear tips, ear moulds, and RIC hearing aids in SNR +5dB conditions.
3. To measure & compare the speech identification scores of subjects fitted with ear tips, ear moulds, and RIC hearing aids in SNR 0 dB conditions.

HYPOTHESIS

The following null hypotheses were formulated for the current study,

1. There would be no significant difference in the speech identification scores of subjects fitted with ear tips, ear moulds & receiver in the canal (RIC) in quiet condition.
2. There would be no significant difference in the speech identification scores of subjects fitted with ear tips, ear moulds & receiver in the canal (RIC) in SNR +5 dB condition.
3. There would be no significant difference in the speech identification scores of subjects fitted with ear tips, ear moulds & receiver in the canal (RIC) in SNR 0 dB condition.

CHAPTER II
REVIEW OF LITERATURE

Hearing Aids are the effective tools for management of different patterns of hearing losses. Now a day, hearing aids come in a variety of shapes and sizes, including traditional behind the ear, in the canal, completely in the canal, and open fit models. Two types of electronics are used in HAs today; they are analog & digital. Analog hearing aids pick up sound waves through a microphone, convert them into electrical signals, amplify them, and send them through the ear canal to the tympanic membrane. Analog hearing aids are less expensive than digital HAs and work on a more linear model of amplification across frequencies. Digital hearing aids allow the implementation of many additional features not possible with analog hearing aids. Fully digital hearing aids can be programmed with multiple programs that can be selected by the user, or that operate automatically and adaptively. These programs reduce acoustic feedback, reduce background noise, detect and automatically accommodate different listening environments, control additional components such as multiple microphones to improve spatial hearing, transpose frequencies (shift high frequencies that a wearer may not be able to hear lower frequency regions where hearing may be better), and implement many other features. Fully digital circuitry also allows control over wireless transmission capability for both the audio and the control circuitry.

Digital hearing aids have several important features potentially not available in a basic linear analog hearing aid, including fine tuning of frequency response, active feedback control, use of multiple channels, multiple microphones and noise reduction strategies. Theoretical advantages of digital over analog amplification are well documented (Dillon, 1996; Hickson, 1994; and Kuk, 1996).

14

Vijayalaxmi (2003) compared the performance of conventional analog and digital hearing aid with trimmer control at different signal to noise ratios. The findings of the study report that speech recognition at -10dB SNR and -20dB SNR inferred that there was a significant difference between analog and digital hearing aids with trimmer control and were better in almost all conditions than analog hearing aids.

Wood (2004) relative benefits of linear analog and advanced digital hearing aids were assessed by matching the speech recognition performance and self-reported benefit in 100 first-time hearing aid users with mild-to-moderate sensorineural hearing loss fitted monaurally with a behind-the-ear (BTE) hearing aid in a single-blind randomized crossover trial. Subjects used each aid for 5 weeks in turn, with aid order balanced across subjects. Aided speech recognition performance was measured at speech levels of 65 and 75dB with speech-to-noise ratio (SNR) of +2dB. Self-rated benefit was measured using the Abbreviated Profile of Hearing Aid Benefit (APHAB) and the Glasgow Hearing Aid Benefit Profile (GHABP).

Speech recognition scores were significantly better for digital hearing aids compared to analog counterpart. Quality of life, hearing aid use & user's preference were also assessed. Findings revealed no significant difference in quality of life between analog and digital aids. However 61 subjects preferred digital aid over analog aid, 26 preferred the analog aid, and 9 being equivocal. Though overall findings it can be concluded that digital hearing aids are better over analog in both subjective & objective measures.

In conclusion it is evident from the studies comparing analog (linear) and digital (non linear) hearing aids that digital hearing aids are superior to analog hearing aids in many ways and owing to its benefits. It is strongly presumable that even for subjects with presbycusis digital hearing aids yield better performance.

Most of the individuals with sensorineural hearing loss have elevated thresholds in the higher frequencies; hence high frequency amplification is certainly the logical approach to remediating their speech-understanding difficulties (Turner, 1999). A number of research studies began to emphasize the importance of providing amplification to frequency regions above 2000Hz (Pasco, 1975 & Skinner, 1980). Amplification options for patients with steeply sloping sensorineural hearing loss in excess of 50 dB per octave are fairly limited (Fabry, Launer & Derleth, 2007). Listener with high-frequency sensorineural hearing loss (HF-SNHL) above 2000Hz present unique amplification challenges. These individuals often exhibit normal hearing sensitivity in the low to mid-frequencies and have been considered marginal.

Sullivan, Allsman, Nielsen, and Mobley (1992) evaluated the effects of various cut-off frequencies in an amplification system, on objective and subjective performance of listeners with steeply sloping, high frequency hearing loss. Non-sense syllable recognition and subjective rating of speech intelligibility and speech quality were obtained from 17 males with bilateral symmetrical high frequency sensorineural hearing loss. Results suggested that syllable recognition increased when additional high frequency information beyond 2 KHz was available; however, the additional amplification was reported to be detrimental to sound quality. Stated differently, performance improved but at the expense of sound quality.

Turner and Henry (2002) reported that listeners with slopping SNHL were able to use amplified high frequency speech information to improve speech understanding when listening in a background of noise regardless of the degree of hearing loss. The results suggested that restoring audibility of

16

high frequency to persons with severe high–frequency SNHL may provide significantly benefit for speech understanding.

Pyler & Fleck (2006) conducted a study to determine if amplifying beyond 2 KHz affected the objective & subjective performance of hearing instruments users with varying degrees of mild-to-severe high frequency SNHL. Two trails were done in which the hearing aid was programmed to maximum high-frequency audibility during one trail period & minimum high frequency audibility during the other trail period & objective evaluation were concluded in quite using the connected speech test (CST) & in noise using the CST & hearing in noise test.

Subjective performance was evaluated by administering the abbreviated profile of hearing aid benefit & questionnaire (APHAB). Results indicated that high frequency amplification significantly improved objective performance in noise & subjective preference in quite for listeners with varying degrees of mild to severe high frequency hearing loss. Results also suggested that high frequency amplification may affect subjective preference in noise & overall for listeners with varying degrees of mild-to-severe high frequency hearing loss when feedback is eliminated.

Beamer, Grand & Walden (2000) examined the effect of high–frequency amplification on subjective benefit in listeners with normal hearing through 2KHz. The profile of hearing aid benefit (PHAB) was administered in the unaided & aided conditions on listeners using BTE or in-the-ear hearing instruments, with linear processing & peak clipping for output limiting (Cox & Rivera, 1992). Results revealed that listeners with normal hearing through 2KHz reported significant subjective benefit for speech communication from high frequency amplification.

The information in the frequencies above 2 KHz is significantly important for understanding speech especially in the presence of noise (Kryter, Williams & Green, 1962). Byrne (1986) reported that listeners with slopping high frequency hearing loss judge the amplification providing the most extended high frequency emphasis to be the poorest in intelligibility. Hogan & Turner (1998) evaluated the effect of hearing loss configuration & severity as well as the frequency bandwidth that maximize speech recognition scores. Speech recognition was tested at various band pass settings for five normal hearing listeners & nine individuals with varying degrees of high frequency hearing loss. The results indicated that for the listeners with normal hearing & individuals with mild high-frequency hearing loss demonstrated an increase in speech recognition scores as audibility increased, whereas individuals with moderate high-frequency hearing losses had poorer scores than the normal hearing individuals and individuals with mild hearing losses.

Turner and Cummings (1999) evaluated the benefit of providing audible speech information to the listeners with high frequency hearing loss. Speech recognition was tested over a wide range of presentation levels for 10 listeners with various degrees & configurations of SNHL. They reported that for listener with a slopping hearing loss, amplifying frequencies beyond 3KHz resulted in little to no improvement in speech recognition scores when hearing loss exceeded 55dBHL. For flat configuration, amplifying frequency beyond 3 KHz resulted in an increase in speech recognition when hearing loss exceeded 55dBHL. These results suggested that benefit obtained from amplifying beyond 3 KHz depends on configuration of loss. The implication of results is that in most cases providing audible speech to lower frequency region will be beneficial. For higher frequency regions in listeners with hearing impairment, amplification may not always be beneficial.

Sullivan, Allsman, Nielsen, & Mohley (1992) studied that increase in speech recognition for listener with flat configuration was contributed to greater gain in the high and mid-frequencies rather than simply amplification beyond 3 KHz. Without amplification, listeners with sloping hearing loss were already receiving maximum mid-frequency speech cues plus some high frequency speech cues. With amplification, listener received only additional high frequency speech cues which resulted in little to no improvement in speech recognition scores. Without amplification, listeners with flat configurations received some mid frequencies and high frequencies speech cues. With amplification, listener with flat configuration received additional mid frequency and high frequency speech cues which resulted in a significant improvement in speech recognition scores. Stated differently, with amplification, listeners with sloping losses were receiving high frequency speech cues, whereas, listeners with flat losses were receiving speech cues in the high frequencies as well as the low to mid frequencies. Therefore, they concluded that improvement in speech recognition scores due to high frequency amplification is questionable. So, alternate solutions to this problem should be developed & changes should be made in the traditional aids.

Open-canal fittings are non-occluding miniature behind the ear (BTE) instruments which are coupled with a thin sound tube and soft, vented silicon ear tip. The tube incorporate a thin wire connected to a receiver located in the ear canal. Open canal fitting represents a two way passage that allows the low frequencies to leak into the residual ear canal without being amplified by the hearing instrument and out of the ear while providing gain in the high frequencies. This results in a much more comfortable fit with a much more natural sound. Furthermore, open canal fitting often have the advantage of being small; have thin tubing and a fashionable design making them a cosmetically appealing (Dillon, 2001; Mueller & Ricketts, 2006). Based on open canal products, cosmetic appeal and their use in fitting mild to moderate high frequency hearing losses, one might assume that the open canal aid's closest competitor would be the completely-in-the canal (CIC) hearing aid of which there are several potential advantages of the open-canal instruments for patient benefits, but elimination of the occlusion effect is the most highly rated (Mueller, 2006). This benefit is also the most highly rated by practitioners dispensing open canal instruments though only a few studies have evaluated the occlusion effect with open-canal instruments (Johnson, 2006).

Many benefits of open canal fittings like improved comfort of fit, cosmetics, sound quality, localization, ease of repair/maintenance, intelligibility, high frequency gain and reduction of the occlusion effect such benefits of open-canal fittings tube that have lead to their rise in popularity (Mueller, 2006). Many of these benefits are a result of the design of these products; leaving the ear canal open allows for air circulation as well as unaltered sound information to enter the ear canal. Recently the open canal hearing aid style has became a viable approach to address many of the problems resulting in non-use of traditional hearing aids, particularly for individuals with mild-moderately severe hearing loss (Mueller, 2006). Although an open canal hearing aid has many potential advantages, there also are potential limitations. The maximum low and high frequency gain available with an open canal fitting is less than that available from traditional custom hearing aid fittings, which could result in less than optical amplification for some individuals. In addition, directional microphone benefits for speech understanding in noise, available with traditional custom fittings, likely will be limited with open canal fittings due to the loss of low frequency gain (Ricketts, Hornsby, & Johnson, 2005). In general the main reason for choosing an open-ear fitting, among many possible reasons, is the minimization or total elimination of the occlusion effect (OE) (Mueller & Ricketts, 2006).

The reduction of OE is possible because the un-occluded ear canal in an open-ear fitting allows the low-frequency sound pressure level that is generated during vocalization to escape through the ear canal. It is commonly accepted that the accumulation of low-frequency SPL during vocalization is the main source of the "hollow voice" complaint. This causes listener to be dissatisfied with the quality of self-generated sounds such as chewing, yawning and most importantly; their own voice (Fagelson & Martin, 1998). The importance of the occlusion effect was observed to with the deepness of insertion of ear moulds (Dean & Martin, 2000). It has been estimated that the average objective occlusion effect with a typical occluding ear mould is about 20dB (Kuk, Keenan, & Peters, 2005). In addition, each 1mm vent diameter leads to a reduction of the OE by 4dB (Kuk, Keenan, & Lau, 2005). This means that, for the average ear to be completely clear of the OE, the equivalent vent diameter of the ear mould should be *larger than 5 mm*. This vent size is almost impossible for a standard custom ITE hearing aid, or a typical ear mould, to achieve. The relationship between the occlusion and feedback effect is dictated by the size of the vent used in the ear moulds (Kiessling, Brenner & Jespersen, 2005). True open-ear fitting is the only possible option to achieve a complete elimination of the objective occlusion effect (Kuk & Keenan, 2006).

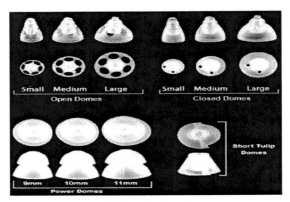

Figure 2.1 shows different types of domes used to provide open fit.

Mueller (2006) in his report on online dispenser survey reported that on an average 17% of all the fittings were open, which suggests that close to 40% of the BTE's being dispensed at the time were open fit. In particular, advances in acoustic feedback reduction algorithms have made modern open canal hearing fittings feasible. Sophisticated feedback reduction algorithms are an integral part of open canal hearing aids, allowing them to provide 8 to 15dB of additional gain before entering the audible oscillatory state (Parsa, 2006). Even in India also, RIC hearing aids are slowly gaining popularity and there is an increase in number of hearing aid prescriptions with RIC hearing aids.

Cox and Alexander (1983) who shown that receiver-in-canal hearing aids attenuate low frequency sounds automatically when the ear is left open (up to 30dB less amplification at 500Hz) especially for hearing in noisy situations. Otto (2005) findings also suggest that receiver-in-canal hearing aids configurations are effective in minimizing the magnitude of the hearing aid occlusion effect and reportedly effective in reducing user perceptions of "hollowness".

A study on the performance of open canal hearing instruments using probe microphone measurements also found maximum gain from the receiver-in-canal instrument at 4 KHz and 6 KHz (Alworth, Plyer, Rebert and Johnstone, 2010). Placement of the receiver deep in the ear canal as in receiver-in-canal fitting permits the individual to benefit from high frequency pinna effects that enhance front-back localization abilities (Van den Bogaert, Carette & Wouters, 2011). Alworth, Plyler, Bertges-Rebert, & Johnstone, (2010) who reported significant performance differences between receiver-in-canal (RIC) hearing aids compared to receiver-in-the-aid (RITA) hearing aids instruments & participants showed significant preference for RIC instruments.

Speech identification score (SIS) is also known as speech recognition score (SRS) or word recognition score (WRS) is a procedure of establishing the percentage of correctly perceived phonetically balanced monosyllabic words or consonant vowel combination presented at a comfortable supra-threshold level. Evaluating SIS is a method in which the subject is presented with a series of stimuli and is asked to identify what he has heard and results are reported in terms of percentage on the basis of correctly repeated words presented to him. The phonetically balanced lists (PB lists) refer to the list of words consisting of a group of single words that were selected so that the frequency of occurrence of speech sounds within a group is same as the frequency of occurrence of the same sound in a language (Kumar & Mohanty, 2012).

Gelfand (2007) has listed the following clinical functions of SIS testing: 1) To describe the extent of hearing impairment in terms of how it affects speech understanding 2) To differentially diagnose auditory disorders by determining the anatomical site of lesion 3) for determining the needs for amplification and other forms of aural rehabilitation devices like cochlear implants, bone anchored hearing aids etc. 4) for making comparisons between various hearing aids, amplification approaches and other forms of aural rehabilitation devices 5) for verifying the benefits of hearing aid use and other forms of aural rehabilitation devices 6) for monitoring patient performance over time for either diagnostic or rehabilitative purpose.

The use of speech identification score (SIS) measures as an effective tool for evaluating the performance of Receiver-In-Canal hearing aid fittings. (Alworth, Plyer, Rebert and Johnstone, 2010) in their study, they have also suggested that objective measures did not show any benefit however subjective measures did indicate aided benefit. During the verification stage of hearing aid, the speech identification scores (SIS) measure allows for one to check out the entire hearing aid and hearing mechanism and during this measurement feedback oscillations are not induced which are obtained often with high gain or deep-fitting hearing aids due to real-ear mic probe placement. It also helps in predicting difficulty the patient might have when communicating in some specific environment when wearing hearing aid as it predicts the speech gain at low speech levels (Hawkins, 2004). Divya (2010) did a comparative study on perceptual & acoustic analysis of speech & music through conventional BTE verses RIC (receiver in the canal) BTE and concluded that speech is processed well through the receiver in the canal (RIC) hearing aid compared to conventional BTE hearing aids.

Prakash, Aparna, Rathna, Madhav, Ashritha & Navyatha (2013) conducted a study to compare the performance of ear tip, ear mould & RIC fittings with digital BTE hearing aids using functional gain measure on ten subject with flat moderately-sever sensorineural hearing loss. Unaided & aided measures were calculated for all fittings at 250 Hz, 500 Hz, 1000 Hz, 2000 Hz & 4000 Hz. Higher scores were obtained with Receiver-In-Canal fitting on Functional gain measures. There was no significant difference between all the three conditions was obtained at low frequencies especially at

24

500 Hz, as RIC hearing aids attenuate low frequency sounds automatically when the ear is left open (up to 30 dB less amplification at 500 Hz) especially for hearing in noisy situations. The results suggest that RIC fittings are an effective means of overcoming the major barriers to the acceptance of amplification including occlusion effect.

To summarize the review, although most of the studies suggested advantages of RIC hearing aid in terms of sound quality, cosmetically, reduction of feedback & elimination of occlusion effect which leads to user satisfaction, there is limited information on the benefit of RIC hearing aid, the present study is being undertaken to evaluate the performance of RIC hearing aids. Review of literature shows that there is difference between the outputs of conventional BTE & RIC hearing aids. Recent studies say that RIC digital hearing aids gives better speech quality than conventional digital BTE. So there is need to check which hearing aid & fitting gives better perception of speech, Hence the present study was taken up.

CHAPTER III
METHODOLOGY

Introduction

The current study was undertaken to evaluate Speech identification scores (SIS) in quiet (without noise mixed), at +5dB and 0dB SNR (signal to noise ratio) conditions using digital BTE hearing aids with different fitting including ear tips, ear moulds & receiver in the canal (RIC) for subjects with bilateral high frequency (sloping) sensorineural hearing loss.

Participants

The data were collected from 30 individuals (15 males & 15 females) with bilateral high-frequency (sloping) sensorineural hearing loss ranging from 20dB to 110dB of air-conduction threshold between frequency range 250 and 8000 Hz (including the inter-octave 3000 Hz) in the age range of 30 to 80 years selected randomly.

Table 3.1 Demographic data of participants

Aspect	Range	Numbers
Age range	30-55 years	10
	55-80 years	20
Educational qualification	Inter completed	20
	Degree holders	05
	Post graduate	05
Gender	Male	15
	Female	15
Hearing loss	Mild to moderate	20
	Moderately-severe	10
Duration of hearing loss	< 3 years	20
	>3 years	10
Hearing aid usage	Nil	Nil

Subject selection criterion

- Adequate speech & language skills.

- Acquired hearing loss.

- No complaint of any neurological problems or middle ear pathology.

- No prior experience with amplification device.

- Native speakers of Telugu language.

- Should not have an air-bone gap greater than 10 dB and not more than 20dB gap in AC thresholds of successive frequencies within the frequency range of 500 to 4000Hz (Kennedy, Levitt, Neumann, & Weiss, 1998).

Test environment

Testing of unaided & aided scores will be carried out in an air conditioned sound treated double room setup, where the ambient noise levels were within the specified limits as recommended by ANSI (1991) standards (cited in Wilber, 2002).

Instructions

The participants were given instructions in Telugu in following way,

"Now, you will hear some words through the loudspeaker. Listen to each word carefully & repeat them as you hear, no matter whether the word is correct or wrong. Whatever you hear, you will have to repeat it loudly, are there any queries?"

Instrumentation

The following instruments were used for data collection,

Hearing aids: two pairs of conventional digital behind the ear (BTE) hearing aids & one pair of receiver in the canal hearing aid of similar features & channels were used. The hearing aids were programmed with a basic fit or first fit using NAL-NL1 prescriptive method and were adjusted as per the client's requirement and satisfaction. All the hearing aids were matched with their technical specifications.

Table 3.2 Features of hearing aids

Characteristics	Receiver in the canal BTE	Conventional BTE
Number of channels	6 channels	6 channels
Maximum output	115dB	115dB
Frequency Response	100-6300 Hz	100-6300 Hz
Full on gain	65dBSPL	65dBSPL
Standard ear hook	Thin wire technology	Yes
Ear mould/ Ear tip	No	Yes

Programming interphase: A computer with NOAH software was used for programming the hearing aids. Hearing aids were connected to the computer using the interface, HIPRO & specific software used to program the hearing aids.

Pure Tone Audiometer: A diagnostic audiometer of LABAT Audiological platform (Audio lab V.4) with free field set up was used for presenting the speech stimuli of phonemically balanced (PB) bi-syllabic word lists of a battery for assessing speech recognition performance of adults in Telugu (Kumar & Mohanty, 2012) in unaided and aided conditions. The output from the laptop was calibrated by using a sound level meter (B & K make 2240 digital SLM) in sound treated room with SLM kept one meter away from the two loud speakers (230 V active speakers). The experiment was conducted in a sound treated free-field setup calibrated as recommended by ANSI (1991).

Test material

A battery for assessing speech recognition performance of adults (Kumar & Mohanty, 2012) was used as a stimulus for determining speech identification scores as a function of different SNR's. The battery consists of four lists of equally difficult disyllabic words with a total of 100 words. These words were constructed based on the frequencies of occurrence of phonemes in Telugu (Rao & Thennarasu, 2007). Out of 100 words, 25 words were selected randomly for the present study. These 25 words were presented randomly at all test conditions to eliminate order & practice effect.

The standardized recorded stimuli with narrow band noise were stored in a personal laptop (Compaq Presario CQ57) which was connected to a calibrated diagnostic audiometer LABAT Audiological platform (Audio lab V.4). The volume control of the speakers and the computer were manipulated such that the output was at the comfortable level of the listener, through the two loud speakers (230 V active speakers).

Data collection procedure

The study was carried out in following technical phases.

Phase I: Selection of participants & hearing aid fitting.

The routine audiological testing which includes pure tone audiometry, speech audiometry & immittance evaluation were carried out for each test ear of each participants. The pure tone audiometry was done by estimating the air conduction thresholds between 250Hz to 8 kHz audiometric frequencies. Those participants satisfying the selection criteria were considered for further evaluation.

The participants seated comfortably on a chair and were fitted with binaural digital BTE hearing aids coupled to test ear using ear tip. Initially, the hearing aids were connected to HIPRO through the appropriate programming cable. The HIPRO was in turn connected to hearing aid specific programming software with a computer and programmed based on NAL-NL1 (Dillon, 1999) prescriptive method and were adjusted as per the client's requirement and satisfaction. All the hearing aids were matched with their technical specifications and programmed separately with ear tips, ear moulds & RIC fittings.

Phase II: Evaluation of Speech identification score (SIS) with ear tips, ear moulds & RIC hearing aid fittings in quiet, SNR +5dB & SNR 0dB conditions.

Evaluation of Speech identification score (SIS) with ear tips, ear moulds & RIC hearing aid fittings will be carried out with standardized speech stimuli with narrow band noise to compare the performance during each fit using a battery for assessing speech recognition performance of adults (Kumar & Mohanty, 2012) in quiet, SNR +5dB & SNR 0dB conditions .The participants were seated comfortably on a chair at a distance of 1 meter from the loudspeakers of the audiometer. The recorded word list along with narrow band noise played on the VLC media player in laptop which was routed through the auxiliary input of the audiometer to the loud speaker. The level of presentation of the stimuli was 70dBHL and level adjustment was done for the calibration tone such that VU-meter deflection averaged at "0".The presentation level of the stimuli was monitored with calibrated tone. The speech identification score was measured by presenting one complete PB word-list of 25 words randomly for each of the three aided conditions. The participant was instructed to repeat the words being presented .The responses were recorded on a response sheet as the number of words correctly identified. Each correct response was given a score of 4% with a maximum score of 100% for each test condition of 25 words. The total number of words correctly repeated in the list was noted. This was considered as the SIS of participants for particular test condition. This procedure was repeated in the three aided conditions, i.e. with ear tips, ear moulds and RIC fittings in quiet, SNR+5dB & SNR 0dB conditions.

Statistical analysis

The data obtained for all the three conditions were computed and analyzed using SPSS software version 17.0. The mean scores and standard deviations for each phase was computed and to explore all possible pair wise comparisons of means, the data was subjected to two-way ANOVA and Post-Hoc analysis in order to find out statistical significance between conditions and within condition. The interpretation of the data is explained in detail in the next chapter.

CHAPTER IV
RESULTS AND DISCUSSION

Introduction

The current study is undertaken to compare the speech identification scores (SIS) of subjects with high frequency sloping hearing loss using digital behind the ear hearing aids fitted with ear tip, ear mould & receiver in the canal (RIC) fittings obtained in quiet, +5dB signal to noise Ratio (SNR) & 0dB signal to noise ratio (SNR) conditions. In this chapter an attempt is made to present the analysis of the data collected for all the three fittings and under three conditions. Further, the data obtained is interpreted and discussed according to the hypothesis formulated for the present study.

Hypothesis-I There would be no significant difference in the speech identification scores of subjects fitted with ear tips, ear moulds & receiver in the canal (RIC) in quiet condition.

Table 4.1 shows the mean and standard deviation values for the SIS with ear tip, ear mould & receiver-in-canal fittings in quiet conditions.

Conditions	Fittings	Mean	Standard eviation(SD)	F - value	Significance
QUIET	ET	74.83	17.29	3.13	0.04*
	EM	77.66	16.49		
	RIC	85.50	17.48		

Note: * - significant difference at p < 0.05 level.

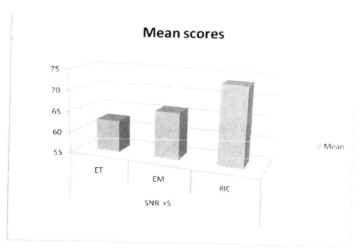

Mean scores

Figure 4.1: Shows the mean and standard deviation values for the SIS with ear tip, ear mould & Receiver-In-Canal fittings in quiet conditions.

The mean speech identification scores (SIS) for receiver-in-canal's fitting was 85.50 (SD=17.48), for ear tip fitting was 74.83 (SD= 17.29) and for ear mould fitting was77.66 (SD=16.49) in quiet condition. It can be noted from the above that receiver-in-canal fitting has the highest mean value as compared to that of ear mould and ear tip fitting as shown in table 4.1 and figure 4.1. The data was further analyzed using two-way ANOVA to establish whether there is a significant difference between fittings in quiet condition, the results revealed significant difference within groups and between fittings with the F-value of 3.13 and significance of 0.04 ($p<0.05$). Hence the null hypothesis stating that "There would be no significant difference in the speech identification scores of subjects fitted with ear tips, ear moulds & receiver in the canal (Receiver-In-Canal) in quiet condition" is rejected.

The results are in accordance with that of Taylor (2006), who reported significantly higher satisfaction ratings of RIC than non BTE hearing aids with regards to sound localization, quality of their own voice, phone comfort and appearance in experienced hearing aid users. It was also noted that the scores at 4 KHz was highest for Receiver-In-Canal fitting.

Hypothesis-II There would be no significant difference in the speech identification scores of subjects fitted with ear tips, ear moulds & receiver in the canal (RIC) in SNR +5dB condition.

Table 4.2: Shows the mean and standard deviation values for the SIS with ear tip, ear mould & RIC fittings in SNR +5dB condition.

Conditions	Fittings	Mean	Standard deviation	F - value	Significance
SNR +5	ET	62.66	14.54	3.89	0.02*
	EM	66.16	15.40		
	RIC	73.50	16.03		

Note: * - significant difference at p < 0.05 level.

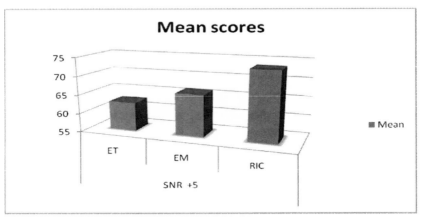

Figure 4.2 shows the mean values for the SIS with ear tip, ear mould & receiver-in-canal fittings in SNR +5dB condition.

The mean speech identification scores (SIS) for receiver-in-canal's fitting was 73.50 (SD=16.03), for ear tip fitting was 62.66 (SD=14.54) and for ear mould fitting was 66.16 (SD=15.40) in +5dB Signal to noise ratio condition. It can be noted from the above that receiver in the canal fitting has the highest mean value as compared to that of ear mould and ear tip fitting as shown in table 4.2 and figure 4.2. The data was further analyzed using two-way ANOVA to establish whether there is a significant difference between fittings in +5dB Signal to noise ratio condition, the results revealed significant difference within groups and between fittings with the F-value of 3.89 and significance of 0.023 ($p<0.05$). Hence the null hypothesis stating that "There would be no significant difference in the speech identification scores of subjects fitted with ear tips, ear moulds & receiver in the canal (RIC) in +5dB Signal to noise ratio condition" is rejected.

The results are similar to the study of Cox and Alexander (1983) who shown that receiver-in-canal hearing aids attenuate low frequency sounds automatically when the ear is left open (up to 30 dB less amplification at 500 Hz) especially for hearing in noisy situations. Otto (2005) findings also suggest that receiver-in-canal hearing aids configurations are effective in minimizing the magnitude of the hearing aid occlusion effect and reportedly effective in reducing user perceptions of "hollowness". This may leads to better speech identification in noise, in current study.

Hypothesis-III There would be no significant difference in the speech identification scores of subjects fitted with ear tips, ear moulds & receiver in the canal (RIC) in SNR 0 dB condition.

Table 4.3 shows the mean and standard deviation values for the SIS with ear tip, ear mould & RIC fittings in SNR 0 dB condition.

Conditions	Fittings	Mean	Standard deviation	F - value	Significance
SNR 0	ET	58.50	13.71	7.272	0.00*
	EM	62.83	14.12		
	RIC	71.16	11.19		

Note: * - significant difference at p < 0.05 level.

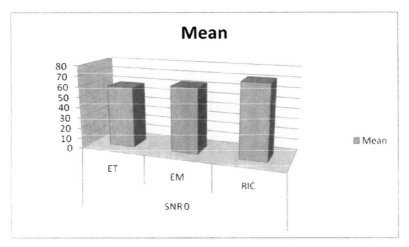

Figure 4.3 shows the mean and standard deviation values for the SIS with ear tip, ear mould & RIC fittings in SNR 0 dB condition.

The mean speech identification scores (SIS) for receiver-in-canal's fitting was 71.16 (SD=11.19), for ear tip fitting was 58.50 (SD=13.71) and for ear mould fitting was 62.83 (SD=14.12) in 0dB Signal to noise ratio condition.

It can be noted from the above that receiver in the canal fitting has the highest mean value as compared to that of ear mould and ear tip fitting as shown in table 4.3 and figure 4.3. The data was further analyzed using two-way ANOVA to establish whether there is a significant difference between fittings in 0dB Signal to noise ratio (SNR) condition, the results revealed significant difference within groups and between fittings with the F-value of 7.272 and significance of 0.001 ($p<0.05$). Hence the null hypothesis stating that "There would be no significant difference in the speech identification scores of subjects fitted with ear tips, ear moulds & receiver in the canal (RIC) in 0dB Signal to noise ratio condition" is rejected.

These findings are in accordance with a study on the performance of open canal hearing instruments using probe microphone measurements also found maximum gain from the receiver-in-canal instrument at 4 KHz and 6 KHz (Alworth, Plyer, Rebert and Johnstone, 2010). Placement of the receiver deep in the ear canal as in receiver-in-canal fitting permits the individual to benefit from high frequency pinna effects that enhance front-back localization abilities (Van den Bogaert, Carette & Wouters, 2011) which may lead to better speech identification scores with RIC fitting in noisy condition in the current study.

To further explore all possible pair wise comparisons of means and to provide specific information on which aspects means are significantly different from each other, the data was subjected to Post-Hoc analysis between fittings i.e. receiver-in-canal, Ear tip and ear mould for all the three conditions.

Table 4.4 shows mean difference, standard error and significance of speech identification scores (SIS) of adults fitted with ear tip, ear mould and receiver-in-canal fitted with hearing aids in quiet, SNR +5 & SNR 0 conditions.

Conditions	Fittings	Mean difference	Standard error	Significance
Quiet	ET Vs EM	2.66	3.72	0.47
	ET Vs RIC	6.00	3.72	0.01*
	EM Vs RIC	8.66	3.72	0.02*
SNR +5	ET Vs EM	3.33	3.68	0.36
	ET Vs RIC	8.16	3.68	0.02*
	EM Vs RIC	11.50	3.68	0.00*
SNR 0	ET Vs EM	4.33	3.53	0.22
	ET Vs RIC	6.83	3.53	0.03*
	EM Vs RIC	11.16	3.53	0.00*

Note: * - significant difference at $p < 0.05$ level. (ET=Ear tube, EM=Ear mould, RIC=Receiver in the canal)

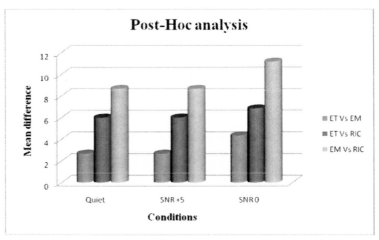

Figure 4.4 Comparison of mean difference of speech identification scores (SIS) of adults fitted with ear tip, ear mould and Receiver-In-Canal fitted with hearing aids in quiet, SNR +5 & SNR 0 conditions.

The results revealed a significant mean difference in ear mould vs. receiver-in-canal fitting (0.02, 0.00 & 0.00, p<0.05) and ear tip vs. receiver-in-canal fittings (0.01, 0.02 & 0.03, p<0.05) in quiet, +5dBSNR and 0dB SNR conditions. However, no significant difference was noted in ear tip vs. ear mould fittings (0.47, 0.36 & 0.22, p<0.05) in quiet, +5dB SNR and 0dB SNR conditions indicating that receiver-in-canal fitting is significant better than ear tip and ear mould fitting in all three conditions and there is no difference in the ear mould and ear tip fittings as shown in the table 4.4.

It can also be noted from the above table that the mean difference between ear mould and receiver in the canal is higher in all three condition with the highest mean difference at +5dB SNR than 0dBSNR and quiet. The mean difference between ear tip & ear mould fitting is low for all the three conditions. Thereby, indicating that RIC fitting is far superior to ear tip & ear mould fitting. These results are supported by the findings of Alworth, Plyler, Bertges-Rebert, & Johnstone, (2010) who reported significant performance differences between receiver-in-canal (RIC) hearing aids compared to receiver-in-the-aid (RITA) hearing aids instruments & participants showed significant preference for RIC instruments.

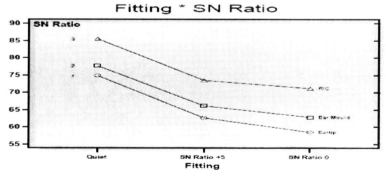

Figure 4.5 Performance of ear tip, ear mould & RIC at three different SNR ratios. (Quiet, +5dB SNR & 0dB SNR)

The findings also indicate that the use of speech identification score (SIS) measures as an effective tool for evaluating the performance of Receiver-In-Canal hearing aid fittings. (Alworth, Plyer, Rebert & Johnstone, 2010) in their study, they have also suggested that objective measures did not show any benefit however subjective measures did indicate aided benefit. During the verification stage of hearing aid, the speech identification scores (SIS) measure allows for one to check out the entire hearing aid and hearing mechanism and during this measurement feedback oscillations are not induced which are obtained often with high gain or deep-fitting hearing aids due to real-ear microphone probe placement. It also helps in predicting difficulty the patient might have when communicating in some specific environment when wearing hearing aid as it predicts the speech gain at low speech levels (Hawkins, 2004). Divya (2010) did a comparative study on perceptual & acoustic analysis of speech & music through conventional BTE verses RIC (receiver in the canal) BTE and concluded that speech is processed well through the receiver in the canal (RIC) hearing aid compared to conventional BTE hearing aids.

Hence, the results concluded that speech identification scores of subjects with high frequency (sloping) hearing loss is higher for RIC fitting. The receiver in the canal (RIC) BTE hearing aid fitting is always superior to ear tips & ear moulds fitting with BTE hearing aid in all three conditions (Quiet, +5 dB SNR & 0d SNR)

CHAPTER V
SUMMARY AND CONCLUSIONS

The present study compared the performance of RIC fitting & traditional fittings with BTE (ear tips & ear moulds fittings) hearing aids in the processing of speech stimuli. The performance was evaluated by comparing speech identification scores with RIC fitting & traditional (ear tips & ear moulds) fittings along with BTE hearing aids in different conditions.

Traditional tube or behind-the-ear (BTE) fittings with ear moulds can alleviate occlusion and insertion loss, may be cosmetically unappealing and present feedback concerns due to the open feedback loop. The advantages of open canal hearing aids suggest that these devices are valuable for individuals in reduction or elimination of the occlusion effect, increased high frequency hearing, a more comfortable physical fit, and the relatively inconspicuous appearance with the potential to increase user satisfaction. Although the performance effects support recommendation of Receiver-In-Canal fittings, clinicians should still consider other factors while discussing options with individual patients. For instance, small ear canals may preclude the use of receiver-in-canal instruments because of retention, comfort or occlusion concerns. Every patient's individual characteristics and concerns must be considered, but the potential benefits of receiver-in-canal instruments warrant further examination.

The data of speech identification scores were collected from 30 individuals with bilateral high-frequency (sloping) sensorineural hearing loss for three fittings (ear tip, ear mould & RIC) in quiet, at SNR +5dB and at 0dB SNR conditions.

Results of the study showed that,

A. There is significant difference in the speech identification scores of subjects fitted with ear tips, ear moulds & receiver in the canal (Receiver-In-Canal) in quiet condition
B. There is significant difference in the speech identification scores of subjects fitted with ear tips, ear moulds & receiver in the canal (RIC) in +5dB signal to noise ratio condition
C. There is significant difference in the speech identification scores of subjects fitted with ear tips, ear moulds & receiver in the canal (RIC) in 0dB Signal to noise ratio condition.
D. There is significant difference in the speech identification scores of subjects between each fit at all conditions.

The results revealed a significant mean difference in ear mould vs. receiver-in-canal fitting and ear tip vs. receiver-in-canal fittings in quiet, +5dBSNR and 0dB SNR conditions. However, no significant difference was noted in ear tip vs. ear mould in all three conditions indicating that receiver-in-canal fitting is significant better than ear tip and ear mould fitting in all three conditions. Results of the study showed that, speech is processed well through the receiver in the canal (RIC) hearing aids compared to traditional fittings with BTE hearing aids (ear tips & ear moulds fittings). This was in agreement with the earlier studies (Kuk, 2008; Hicks, Dawkes, Michael, Nilsson, 2009)

The results of this study on the speech identification measures provide data base outside hearing aid companies, and were consistent with other studies, and suggest that open canal fittings (RIC) are an effective means of overcoming one of the major barriers to the acceptance of amplification: poor own-voice sound quality resulting from the hearing aid occlusion effect. The results can be used in the rehabilitation of hearing impaired individuals with moderately severe to severe (sloping) SN hearing losses by providing hearing aids that will provide maximum benefit to them.

Clinical implication of the study

This study provides documentation regarding the speech identification scores using different fittings with digital hearing aids in different conditions. The following clinical implications can be derived from the present study which may be useful for Audiologists, and hearing aid manufacturers especially when considering hearing aid fitting for the elderly hearing impaired population.

➢ This information is critical for Audiologists when counselling clients regarding the available fitting options with hearing aids and advantages them in noisy conditions.

➢ The present study suggests that the Audiologist should use the speech audiometric procedures for evaluating, selecting and fitting of a hearing aid for subjects with hearing loss.

➢ The separation of receiver from the body of the BTE hearing aid is the most advanced technology to provide more gain specifically at high frequencies and management of feedback is highly essential for amplification devices in individuals with high frequency sloping hearing loss.

➢ Open fit RIC hearing aid is the best solution for individuals with normal or minimal low frequency hearing loss for reduction of occlusion effect and comfort sound quality than providing venting option in custom ear mould with BTE hearing aids.

➢ This study helps the Audiologist to reduce the time taken for hearing aid fitting especially in elderly subjects who cannot patiently wait for longer testing times due to their physiological fatigue.

➢ This study suggest that performance of hearing aid increases with receiver in the canal fitting compared to ear tip & ear mould fittings, hence for the hearing aids manufacturers it is important to consider alternatives to make the higher end hearing aid's performance superior over the other fittings, as the higher end hearing aids are more expensive than the other hearing aids.

➢ It is important to consider hearing aid trial in quiet condition as well as in the presence of background noise as the natural communication situation does not imitate the quiet condition and as it was evident from the current study that there is large difference in the speech identification score in quiet situation compared to that of different SNR conditions.

Limitations of the study

➢ The tests in the study were laboratory type experiments and conducted without any prior hearing aid trial period. They may lead to an underestimation of the performance of the hearing aids used as acclimatization is not achieved towards the hearing aid.

➢ One cannot assume that the findings in this investigation are comparable to "real world" performance with this device. Although attempts have been made to simulate the "real world" environment by utilizing noise, the conditions utilized in this study are still not typical of "real world" listening environments and speech identification testing was conducted in a sound treated environment, which results in reduced effects from reverberation.

➢ Speech identification scores were obtained at one fixed level (70dBHL) in quiet, at SNR +5dB and at 0dB SNR conditions. Speech identification scores should have been obtained at a range of noise levels which may provide more useful information about the hearing aid performance.

➢ This study did not use the period of acclimatization to measure the speech identification scores.

➤ This study used disyllables as the stimulus. Speech identification scores using words or sentences would be more beneficial.

Recommendations for further research

➤ Further studies have to be done with different types of noise and diffuse listening conditions to understand the effect of this receiver in the canal hearing aid's technology in real life situations.

➤ Further studies have to be done with different types of noise and diffuse listening conditions with objective evaluation (real ear gain measures) to study the performance of receiver in the canal hearing aid's technology in real life situations.

➤ A further study using self rating scales and questionnaires in combination with the measures of obtaining speech identification scores in quiet and noise conditions can be carried out.

➤ A further study measuring the speech recognition scores at various S/N ratios will help us know more about the performance of RIC with the hearing aid in real life situations.

➤ A further study to measure the speech identification scores at regular intervals of time would help us to know the benefit with the hearing aid after a certain period of acclimatization.

➤ A further study using multichannel RIC hearing aids with more than 12 channels would help us to know the effects of increasing number of channels beyond 12.

➤ It could also be beneficial if an experimental aid with different open fitting could be included in the future studies for baseline a comparison.

➤ It could also be beneficial if the improvement in speech identification scores from unaided to linear and nonlinear multichannel hearing aids which would give an estimation of quantitative effect of increasing number of channels in RIC hearing aids.

> Only when the bridge between perceptual assessment and hearing aid architecture narrows will we achieve success in adequately fitting different signal processing strategies.
> It could also be beneficial to use sentences as the stimulus material in order to assess real communication difficulties with RIC hearing aids.

In conclusion the present study evaluated the speech identification scores (SIS) in 30 subjects with high frequency sloping hearing loss fitted with traditional fitting (ear tip & ear mould) & RIC hearing aids. The results of the study revealed that there is significant difference between RIC BTE hearing aid fitting compared with ear tip & ear mould fitted with BTE hearing aids and compared in quiet, +5dB SNR & 0dB SNR condition. There is no significant difference between ET Vs EM fittings with BTE hearing aids in all three conditions. Significant difference was found in all the conditions for ET Vs RIC & EM Vs RIC fittings with BTE hearing aids i.e. in quiet condition the subjects performed better over the noise condition.

REFERENCES

American National Standards Institute, Specifications for Pure Tone Audiometers (ANSI S 3.6- 1969), Author, New York, 1970.

American Speech and Hearing Association (1988). Guidelines for Manual Pure-Tone Threshold Audiometery, *ASHA*, 20, 297-301.

American National Standard Institute (1991). American National Standard maximum permissible ambient noise levels in audiometric test rooms. *ANSI, S 3.1* New York.

Alworth, L. N., Plyer, P. N., Rebert M. N. & Johnstone, P. M. (2010). The Effect of Receiver Placement on Probe Microphone Performance and Subjective Measures with Open Canal Hearing Instruments, *Journal of the American Academy of Audiology*,21(4), 249-266.

Beamer, S.L., Grant, K.W., & Walden, B.E. (2000).Hearing aids benefit in patient with high frequency hearing loss. *Journal of the American Academy of Audiology*, 11, 429-437.

Byrne, D. (1986). Effect of frequency response characteristics on speech discrimination. *Journal of the Acoustical Society of America, 80, 494-504.*

Christensen, L. & Matsui, G. (2003). Hearing Aid Satisfaction with ReSound Air, GN Resound White Paper.

Chung, k., Neuman, A. & Higgins, M. (2005) Effects of In The-Ear Microphone Directionality on Sound Direction Identification, *Journal of the Acoustical Society of America*, 123(4), 2264-2275.

Cox, R. M., & Alexander, G. C. (1983). Acoustic versus Electronic Modifications of Hearing Aid Low Frequency Output, *Ear and Hearing*, 4(4), 190-196. Doi:10.1097/00003446-198307000-00003.

Cox, R. M., & Rivera, I.M., (1992). Predictability & reliability of hearing aid benefit measured using the PHAB. *Journal of the American Academy of Audiology*, 3, 242-254.

Dean, M.S., & Martin, F.N. (2000). Insert earphone depth & the occlusion effect. *American Journal of Audiology*, 9, 131-134.

Dillon, H. (1999). NAL-NAL 1, *Journal of the American Academy of Audiology*, 10 (1), 60-69.

Dillon, H. (2001). Hearing Aids: Hearing Aid Earmolds, Earshells, and Coupling Systems, Boomerang Press, Sydney.

Dillon, H., Birtles, G., & Lovegrove, R. (1999). Measuring the Outcomes of a National Rehabilitation Program: Normative Data for the Client Oriented Scale of Improvement (COSI) and the Hearing Aid User's Questionnaire (HAUQ), *Journal of the American Academy of Audiology*,10(2),67-79.

Divya,S.J. (2010). A comparative study on perceptual & acoustic analysis of speech & music through conventional BTE verses RIC (receiver in the canal). *Unpublished Master's Dissertation, Mysore*, University of Mysore.

Durrer, K. (2008). Critical Review: In Individuals with Sensorineural Hearing Loss, Are There Benefits of Open Canal Hearing Aid Fittings Relative to

Those of Traditional Fittings? *Candidate School of Communication Sciences and Disorders*,2008.

Fabry, D.A., Launcer, S., & Derleth, P. (2007). Hearing aid technology Vs. steeply sloping sensorineural hearing loss, *Hearing Review*. 10 (2), 12-19.

Flynn, M.C., Obleing, L., & Johnson, J.,(2006). Thin tube open fittings: preferred patient populations & study results. *Hearing Review*, 13 (3), 62-95.

Gelfand, S. A. (2007). Speech Audiometry: *In Essentials of Audiology, 2nd Ed*, Thieme Medical Publishers, New York.

Gnewikow, D., & Moss, M. (2006). Hearing Aid Outcomes with Open and Closed Canal Fittings, *Hearing Journal*, 59(11), 66-72.

Griffing, T. S. & Preves, D. P. (1976) In-the-Ear Aids, Part I, *Hearing Instruments*, 27(3), 22-24.

Hawkins, D. (2004). Limitations & Uses of Aided Audiogram, *Seminars in Hearing*, 25(1), 51-62. Doi:10.1055/s-2004-823047.

Hicks, M. L., Dawkes, A.H., Nilson, M. J. (2009). *An article downloaded from sonic innovations.*

Hogen, C.A., & Turner, C.W. (1998). High-frequency audibility. *Journal of the Acoustical Society of America*, 104, 432-442.

Jespersen, C., Groth, J., Kiessling, J., Brenner, B.,Jensen, O. (2006). The Occlusion Effect in Unilateral versus Bilateral HearingAids. *Journal of American Academy of Audiology*,17(4), 763-773.

Johnson, E. E. (2006). Segmenting Dispensers: Factors in Selecting Open-Canal Fittings, *Hearing Journal*, 59(11), 58-64.

Kennedy,E., Levitt, H.,Neuman, A.C.,& Weiss, M.,(1998). Consonant-Vowel intensity ratios for maximizing consonant recognition by hearing-impaired listeners. *Journal of the Acoustical Society of America*, 103 (2), 1098-1114.

Kiessling, J., Brenner, B., Jespersen, C.T., Grouth J. (2005). Occlusion effect of earmoulds with different venting systems. *Journal of the American Academy of Audiology 16(4), 237-49.*

Kiessling J., Brenner B., Jespersen, C. T. (2005). Occlusion Effect of Earmolds with Different Venting Systems, *Journal of the American Academy of Audiology*, 16(4),237-249. Doi:10.3766/jaaa.16.4.5

Kiessling, J., Margolf-Hackl, S. & Gellar, S. (2001). Field Test of an Occlusion-Free Hearing Instrument, *GN ReSound White Paper.*

Killion, M. C., Wilber, L. A., & Gudmundsen, G. I. (1988). A Potential Solution for the "Hollow Voice" Problem (the Amplified Occlusion Effect) with Deeply Sealed Earmolds, *Hearing Instruments*, 39(1), 14-18.

Kuk, F., Ludvigsen, C. (2002) Ampclusion management 101: Understanding variables. *Hearing Review,* 9(8), 22-32.

Kuk, F., Keenan, M., & Ludvigsen, C. (2005). Efficacy of an Open-Fitting Hearing Aid, *Hearing Review*, 12(2), 26-32.

Kuk, F., Keenan, M., & Peeters, (2005). Efficacy of an Open-Fitting Hearing Aid, *Hearing Review*, 12(2), 26-32.

Kuk, F. & Keenan, D. (2006). An Open-Fitting Hearing Aid, *Hearing Review*, 13(2), 34-42.

Kuk, F. (2008). Efficacy of an Open-Fitting Hearing Aid, *Hearing Review*, 12(2), 26-32.

Kuk, F. & Backgard , L., (2008).Hearing aid selection & BTE: choosing among various open ear & receiver in the canal options. *Hearing review.*15 (13),22-36.

Kumar, S. B., & Mohanty, P. (2012). Speech Recognition Performance of Adults: A Proposal Battery for Telugu. Centre for Applied Linguistics and Translation Studies, University of   Hyderabad, INDIA.

Lenvins, B.L. (1996)The future and the young-old. *The Gerentologist*, 15, 4-9.

MacKenzie, D. J., Mueller, H. G., Ricketts, T. A. & Konkle, D. F. (2004). The Hearing Aid   Occlusion Effect: A Comparison of Two Measurement Devices, *Hearing Journal*,   57(9), 30-39.

Mueller, H.G., Bright, K.E., Northern, J.L. (1996). Studies of the hearing aid occlusion effect. *Seminars in Hearing*, 17(1), 21-32.

Mueller, H. G., (2003). Page Ten: There's Less Talking in Barrels, but the Occlusion Effect is Still with us," *Hearing Journal*, 56(8),10-16.

Mueller, H.G. (2006) Open is in. *Hearing Journal,* 59(11), 11-14.

Mueller, H. G., & T. A., Ricketts, (2006). Open-Canal Fittings: Ten Take Home Tips, *Hearing Journal*, 59(11), 24-39.

Noble, W., Sinclair, S., Byrne, D. (1998). Improvement in Aided Sound Localization with Open Ear moulds: Observations in People with High-Frequency Hearing Loss. *Journal of American Academy of Audiology*, 9, 25-34.

Otto, W. (2005) Evaluation of an Open Canal Hearing Aid by Experienced Users, *Hearing Journal*, 58(8), 26-32.

Painton, S. W., (1993). Objective Measure of Low-Frequency Amplification Reduction in Canal Hearing Aids with Adaptive Circuitry, *Journal of the American Academy of Audiology*, 4 (3), 152-156.

Parsa, V. (2006). Acoustic Feedback and Its Reduction through Digital Signal Processing, *The Hearing Journal*, 59(11), 16-23.

Pascoe, D.P., (1975). Frequency response of hearing aids & Their effects on speech perception of hearing-*Annals of Otology, Rhynology & Laryngology*, 84(23),5-40.

Plyler, P.N., & Fleck, E.,L. (2006). The effect of high-frequency amplification on the degree of high frequency hearing loss.*Journal of Speech, Language & Hearing Research*, 49 (3), 616-627.

Prakash, S. G. R., Aparna, R., Rathna S. B., Madhav, T., Ashritha, K., Navyatha, K. (2013). Sensori-Neural Hearing Loss Client's Performance with Receiver-In-Canal (RIC) Hearing Aids, *International Journal of Otolaryngology and Head & Neck* Surgery, 2, 68-73. doi:10.4236/ijohns.2013.22017.

Rao, G. U. & Thenarasu, S. (2007). PGDCAIL: CAIL-421. Corpus Linguistics, University of Hyderabad.

Ricketts,T.,Hornsby, B., & Johnson,E.,(2005). Adaptive directional benefit in the near field. *Seminars in Hearing. 26(2), 59-69.*

Ross, M., &Cirmo, R. (1980). Reducing feedback in post auricular hearing aid by implanting receiver in the ear mould. *Volta Review,* 40-44.

Staab, W. & Lyberger (1994)." Digital Hearing Aids". *Hearing Instruments.* 31(7), 14-25.

Sullivan, J.A., Allsman,C.S., Nielson,C.B. & Mobley, J.P.(1992).Amplification for listeners with steeply sloping high frequency hearing loss. *Ear and Hearing,* 13(1),35-45.

Sweetow, R. W. & Pirzanski, C. W., (2003). The Occlusion Effect and Ampclusion Effect. *Seminars in Hearing,* 24(4), 333-344. Doi: 10.1055/s-2004-815549.

Taylor, B. (2006). Real-World Satisfaction and Benefit with Open-Canal Fittings, *Hearing Journal*, 59(11), 74-82.

Turner, C.W., & Cummings, K.J. (1998). Speech audibility for listener with high-frequency hearing loss, *American Journal of Audiology*, 8, 1-10.

Turner, C.W. (1999). Limits of high-frequency amplification. *Hearing Journal*, 53 (2), 10-14.

Turner, C.W., & Henry, B., (2002). Benefits of amplification in back ground noise. *Journal of Acoustic Society of America*, 112, 1675-1680.

Van den Bogaert, T., Carette, E. & Wouters, J. (2011). Sound Source Localization Using Hearing Aids with Microphones Placed 8Behind-The-Ear, in-the-Canal, and in- the Pinna, *International Journal of Audiology*, 50(3), 164-176.

Vijayalaxmi (2003). A Comparative Study of Performance with Conventional analog digital Hearing Aid with Trimmer Control at Different Signal to Noise Ratio. *An unpublished Independent project Submitted on part fulfillment of M.Sc (Speech and Hearing)*, University of Mysore, Karnataka, India.

Wood, S., and Lutman, M. (2004). Relative benefits of linear analog and advanced digital hearing aids. *International Journal of Audiology*, 43, 144-155.

Appendix I
Final word List (Adults)

N	List 1		List 2		List 3		List 4	
1	పాత	pāta	కోతి	kōti	పాట	pāṭa	తోట	tōṭa
2	నేను	nēnu	గోడ	gōḍa	కూర	kūra	నూనె	nūne
3	యాస	yāsa	రేటు	rēṭu	జాలి	jāli	రైతు	raitu
4	జేబు	jēbu	బాతు	bātu	ఎది	ĕdi	వెడి	wĕḍi
5	పేరు	pēru	గాలి	gāli	నోరు	nōru	నీకు	nīku
6	లేదు	lēdu	దారి	dāri	కోడి	kōḍi	షాపు	ṣāpu
7	కాలు	kālu	తెలు	tēlu	లైటు	laiṭu	గోరు	gōru
8	తేనె	tēne	నాకు	nāku	షోకు	ṣōku	లేడు	lēḍu
9	రౌడి	rauḍi	సెవ	sēwa	వాడు	wāḍu	కాశీ	kāśī
10	వాన	wāna	రోలు	rōlu	మూల	mūla	రాను	rānu
11	షాకు	ṣāku	నిడ	nīḍa	చీర	cīra	సైగ	saiga
12	మీరు	mīru	కసి	kasi	గౌను	gaunu	పాలు	pālu
13	సూది	sūdi	నూరు	nūru	దోశ	dōśa	లారి	lāri
14	చాలు	cālu	జోకు	jōku	రైలు	railu	నాది	nādi
15	మేక	mēka	శని	śani	మేత	mēta	చాట	cāṭa
16	టివి	ṭīwi	చెయి	cĕyi	నస	nasa	నెల	nela
17	వాగు	wāgu	దోమ	dōma	ఊరు	ūru	సరే	sarē
18	కోటు	kōṭu	షాపు	ṣāpu	బోను	bōnu	మాట	māṭa
19	లోయ	lōya	నెల	nēla	ఎటు	eṭu	వాత	wāta
20	దారు	cāru	రాయి	rāyi	పూస	pūsa	బావ	bāwa
21	పైన	paina	పాము	pāmu	నీతి	nīti	మాయ	māya
22	మూడు	mūḍu	విను	winu	మూగ	mūga	జామ	jāma
23	లేను	lēnu	టోపి	ṭōpi	తోక	tōka	పీక	pīka
24	రాశి	raśi	చీమ	cīma	విపు	wīpu	చెడు	cĕdu
25	తిగ	tīga	వోటు	wōṭu	చేను	cēnu	కాయ	kāya

\# In Telugu, the words beginning with front vowels /i/, /ī/, /e/ & /ē/ are preceded by the palatal glide /y/ and back vowels /u/, /ū/, /o/ and /ō/ are preceded by labial glide /w/ when they occur in initial position. Hence, the words in the lists /ūru/, /eṭu/ and /ĕdi/ are considered as [wūru], [yeṭu] and [yĕdi] respectively in this study.

CPSIA information can be obtained
at www.ICGtesting.com
Printed in the USA
LVOW11s1152140217
524218LV00001B/129/P

9 783659 128509